Broomsticks
and
Balloons

Science Experiments Using Everyday Objects

Jenny Lachlan

Heinemann Educational Publishers
Halley Court, Jordan Hill, Oxford OX2 8EJ
a division of Reed Educational & Professional Publishing Limited

Heinemann is a registered trademark of Reed Educational & Professional Publishing Limited

OXFORD   MELBOURNE   AUCKLAND
JOHANNESBURG   BLANTYRE   GABORONE
IBADAN   PORTSMOUTH (NH) USA   CHICAGO

First published 1999

03 02 01 00 99
10 9 8 7 6 5 4 3 2 1

British Library Cataloguing in Publication Data
A catalogue record for this book is available from the British Library.

ISBN 0 435 09675 3   *Broomsticks and Balloons* single copy

ISBN 0 435 09676 1   *Broomsticks and Balloons* 6 copy pack

Acknowledgements
All photographs by Rupert Horrox
All illustrations by Hardlines
Printed and bound in the UK

Contents

Home-made compass

A compass is a direction-finding instrument, with a needle that always points towards north. This experiment shows you how to make a simple compass.

Equipment

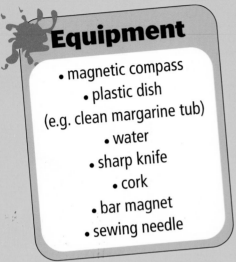

- magnetic compass
- plastic dish (e.g. clean margarine tub)
- water
- sharp knife
- cork
- bar magnet
- sewing needle

Method

1. Use the compass to find north, and make a note of this information.
2. Fill the plastic dish with water.
3. Use the knife to slice off a thin piece of cork, about 5 mm thick. ⚠ Ask an adult to help.
4. Float the piece of cork in the water.
5. Rub one end of the magnet along the needle about 75 times, stroking in one direction only.
6. Carefully lay the needle on top of the cork.
7. Observe the direction in which the needle points.
8. Compare your findings with the original compass reading.

Like poles repel one another.

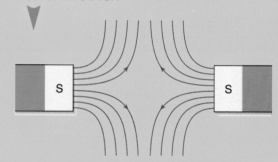

Unlike poles attract one another.

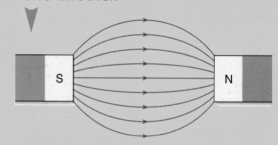

Why does this happen?

All magnets have two poles. These are called the north pole and the south pole. If the north pole of one magnet is put next to the north pole of another magnet, the two magnets will repel, or push against, one another. The same thing happens if two south poles are put together. But if a north pole is put next to a south pole, the two magnets attract, or pull towards, each other.

Compasses work because the Earth acts like a huge magnet. The south pole of a magnet is attracted to the north pole of the Earth. By rubbing the magnet along the needle, the needle is turned into a magnet. Placing the needle on a piece of cork in water enables it to move freely. So one end of the needle, its south pole, spins around to point towards north.

Electric hair

Have you ever wondered why your hair sometimes stands on end? This experiment shows you how it can be done.

Equipment

- balloon
- woollen jumper or glove

Method

1. Blow up the balloon and tie a knot at the end.
2. Rub the balloon up and down on the jumper or glove.
3. Hold the balloon away from your body and gradually bring the balloon towards your head.
4. Hold the balloon steadily and observe what happens to your hair. What kind of sensation do you feel in your hair?

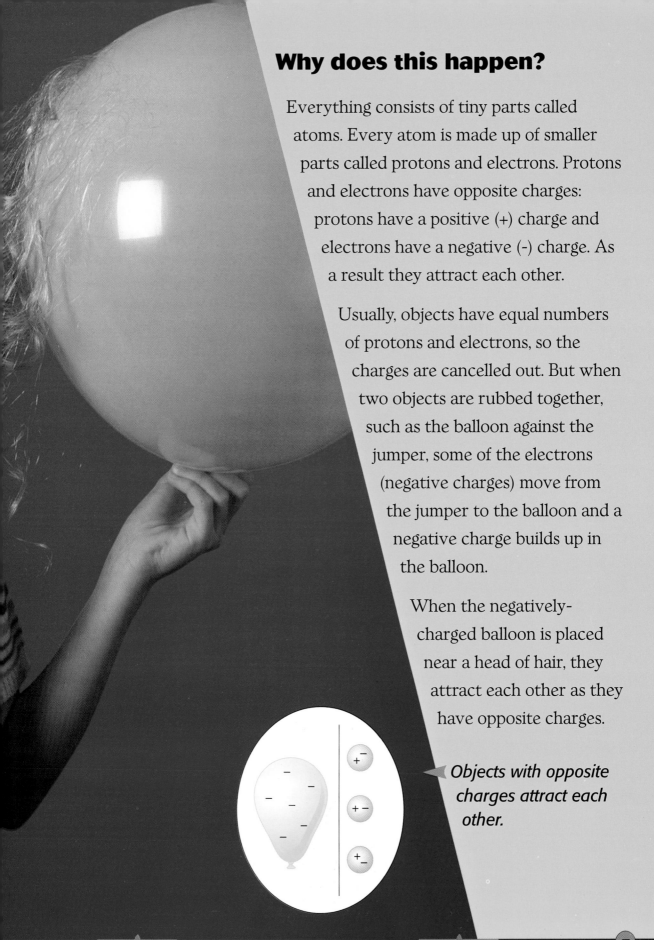

Why does this happen?

Everything consists of tiny parts called atoms. Every atom is made up of smaller parts called protons and electrons. Protons and electrons have opposite charges: protons have a positive (+) charge and electrons have a negative (-) charge. As a result they attract each other.

Usually, objects have equal numbers of protons and electrons, so the charges are cancelled out. But when two objects are rubbed together, such as the balloon against the jumper, some of the electrons (negative charges) move from the jumper to the balloon and a negative charge builds up in the balloon.

When the negatively-charged balloon is placed near a head of hair, they attract each other as they have opposite charges.

Objects with opposite charges attract each other.

Leaf masks

All living things need food to survive. Unlike animals, plants cannot eat, so they need to make their own food. This experiment shows how plants obtain their food.

Equipment

- sheet of cardboard
- scissors
- pot plant with large leaves
- paper clips

Method

1. Cut some interesting shapes, smaller than the size of the leaves of the plant, out of the cardboard. These are the masks.

2. Attach each mask to the upper surface of a leaf using a paper clip. Be careful not to pierce the leaf.

3. Position the plant in sunlight, but ensure that it does not become overheated. Keep the soil moist by watering it.

4. After a week, remove the masks. Observe any changes in the leaves.

Why does this happen?

Plants use substances in the air and soil to make food. They take in carbon dioxide gas through their leaves, and water through their roots. Then, using the energy in sunlight, they turn the carbon dioxide and water into a type of sugar called glucose. This is their food. This food-making process is called photosynthesis (photo means 'light', and synthesis means 'making new substances').

The green colouring matter in plants is called chlorophyll. Plants use this substance to absorb the energy from the sun.

When a leaf is deprived of light, as in the area under the mask, the plant is no longer able to make food there. The leaf does not need water supplied to it, so the plant closes off tiny tubes in the base of the leaf which carry water from the stem. Chlorophyll needs fresh water to renew itself. Without water it will disappear from the leaf, taking the green colour with it.

Broomstick pulley

Do you think it is possible for one person to overcome the combined strength of two others? Here's an experiment that shows you how it can be done.

Equipment

- two friends
- two broomsticks
- rope (about 3 m long)

Method

1. Ask each friend to hold a broomstick vertically and to stand facing each other about 1 m apart.

2. Tie one end of the rope to one broomstick.

3. Wind the free end of the rope around the other broomstick, then wind it back around the first broomstick. Continue to wind the rope around both broomsticks several times, as shown in the photograph.

4. Hold on to the free end of the rope, and stand next to one of your friends.

5. Ask your friends to lift the broomsticks off the floor and to try to hold the broomsticks apart while you try to pull them together.

6. Pull steadily on the rope. Who is more successful, you or your friends?

Why does this happen?

The rope and the broomsticks act as a pulley. A pulley is a simple machine that increases the force exerted by your muscles. Every time the rope is wound around a broomstick, your pulling force is magnified. Each section of rope pulls on the broomsticks with the same amount of force as you are putting into pulling the rope. So the force exerted on the rope is as if six people are pulling. This means that you are probably able to pull the broomsticks together, overcoming the effort of the two people who are trying to pull them apart.

Worm farm

All living things need food to live and grow.
This experiment shows what happens
when worms start eating.

Equipment

- large, wide-mouthed jar
- garden soil or potting compost (enough to half fill the jar)
- water spray
- sand (enough to half fill the jar)
- apple and carrot peelings (about a cupful)
- four earthworms
- sheet of black sugar paper
- tape

Method

1. Spread a layer of soil 2.5 cm deep in the bottom of the jar. Moisten the soil using the water spray.
2. Add a 2.5 cm deep layer of sand. Continue to add more layers of soil and sand until the surface is 5 cm from the top of the jar. Fill the rest of the jar with apple and carrot peelings.
3. Place the worms on top of the peelings. Remember to handle the worms carefully.
4. To stop light from entering the glass, tape the sugar paper tightly around the outside of the jar.
5. Put the jar in a dark place for three days.
6. After three days, remove the sugar paper. Does the worm farm look any different? Record your findings.
7. Replenish the food in the jar by adding some more peelings. Remoisten the soil using the water spray.
8. Replace the sugar paper and return the jar to a dark place for a further three days.
9. After three days, remove the sugar paper. How does the worm farm look now? Record your findings and compare them with your previous observations.
10. When you have finished observing your worm farm, empty the contents of the jar into a patch of soil.

Why does this happen?

Earthworms are part of nature's way of fertilising the soil. The peelings and other food they eat are broken down as they pass through their digestive systems. The food wastes are deposited in the soil as casts. The casts help to enrich the soil.

Bottle balloon

How can you make a balloon inflate without using your mouth? Try this experiment and see.

Equipment

- balloon
- large empty plastic bottle
- 2 large bowls
- hot water (enough to half fill one of the bowls)
- ice (enough to half fill one of the bowls)

Method

1. Fit the balloon securely over the mouth of the plastic bottle.
2. Carefully pour the hot water into one bowl. ⚠ Ask an adult to help.
3. Put the ice into the other bowl.
4. Stand the bottle with the balloon in the bowl of hot water for a few seconds. Observe what happens.
5. Remove the bottle from the hot water and transfer it to the bowl of ice. Observe what happens to the balloon this time.

Why does this happen?

Although the bottle looks empty, it is actually full of air molecules. These molecules constantly move around inside the bottle. When air is heated, the molecules move faster. So when the bottle with the balloon is put into the hot water, the molecules in the bottle move faster. This means that they bounce off the inside of the balloon more often, forcing it to expand. When the bottle with the balloon is put into the ice, the balloon deflates, or collapses, because the molecules slow down and do not hit the sides as often.

Index